we
find
our
way.

Also by Reyna Biddy

I Love My Love

A Psalm for Us

WE FIND OUR WAY

north node

reyna biddy

Andrews McMeel
PUBLISHING®

Andrews McMeel Publishing
a division of Andrews McMeel Universal
1130 Walnut Street, Kansas City, Missouri 64106

www.andrewsmcmeel.com

22 23 24 25 26 VEP 10 9 8 7 6 5 4 3 2 1

ISBN: 978-1-5248-73868

Library of Congress Control Number: 2022933819

Editor: Patty Rice
Art Director: Holly Swayne
Production Editor: Brianna Westervelt
Production Manager: Cliff Koehler

ATTENTION: SCHOOLS AND BUSINESSES
Andrews McMeel books are available at quantity discounts with bulk purchase
for educational, business, or sales promotional use. For information,
please e-mail the Andrews McMeel Publishing Special Sales Department:
specialsales@amuniversal.com.

for umi.

you matter the most to me.
who you become in this life
who you were before you got here
how i can best assist you to reach
your next destination. so i start with
love, as always. you are in safe hands.
i trust you,   do you trust me?

you are a reflection
of everything
i've ever loved.
and everyone who's ever
meant the world to me.

my soul mate. it's nice
to meet   you again.

contents

we
find
our
way.

OPEN

The melancholy of my life seems to be well balanced
with the breeding of joy; whether i am to be on
the giving or receiving end. I'm compelled to
produce a love that's intimate, between you and I.
The uncertainty of my life has become humorous.
Mocking even. Followed by signs, lights, numbers,
wind, water, birds—I surrender. I am holy. I am
magic. I affirm it to be true. When it's my time to
work, I have no choice. When it's my turn to pour,
I give myself. I recognize the obligations set on
my life, I must search for the truth, then tell it. I
understand the responsibilities that come with the
gift of believing. Sometimes it's easier to be a fool.
One might believe, when you live in the unknown
you keep your sanity—your soul even. I've made a
contract with spirit. I understand what's expected of
me. Voice, laughter, song. To stay aware, and alive, is
no easy task. This world wasn't groomed for survival.
We show ourselves, then we disappear, only to be
reborn again. But to whose jurisdiction? Human?
I've grown tired of human shit. I'd like to choose
my heaven, and settle in. Our return mustn't be so
redundant. How dreadful to start over . . . and over
and over again. I spread myself thin, if it means i'll
be rewarded.
The return varies.
I cannot confirm or deny the luxuries.

To see through all things. To see all things so deeply.
   A harsh power one can hope for,
      and regret at the same time.

When i first began writing poetry it was an effortless
duty. I'd form words and create stories, pulling from
both feelings and experiences, that were no longer
a reality in the present. Often i go back and i don't
remember anything. 20 years of purging—well done.
At 26 I have no recollection. The thing about me
is, after i grieve, i isolate myself from the process
of healing. I only take my badge with me. Moving
forward, and beyond, toward the next process. onto
the next project. then again.

   I wish it were easier to sit still.

student things

you think you know

discipline, patience,
empathy, and strength..
until you give birth
to your teacher.

help me sing

what i've learned
is, i discern best in
the dark. it's hard
to be candid
under bright lights

what i've learned
is distractions don't
always come in flesh.
heartbreak
doesn't always
come with healing.
holding grudges
for a moment,
adds more lives to you.
the karma brings
you back a few times.

tears cleanse the soul.

pain is a magnet
pay attention to
what attracts to you.
pay attention to
what y'all birth.
pay attention
to your baby.
you gave her life.

master lessons

you cannot evolve
while holding onto
those who are incapable.

in this life

we tend to get caught up in the aesthetic of things.
we learn to care about reputation before self
preservation. we fall in love behind closed doors. we
laugh at jokes that we could never say aloud—due
to the fear of being seen. scared to be ourselves.
scared being ourselves will never make the cut. at
some point, we became too serious. we've labeled
everything as problematic. we've forgotten how to
mind the business that pays us. i've learned to be
accepting of it all. the love, the hate, the neglect, the
skepticism, the criticism, the praise, and everything
in between. i've never cared to be anyone's favorite.
i don't believe i'm here for that. my purpose is
quite simple. break generational curses. escape
generational trauma. speak the truth—as i know it.
share my journey as i go. give reference and resources
if possible. connect the dots for others. connect
others—with each other. be a source of light. raise a
village with, and of, love. leave control behind. leave
judgment behind. leave baggage behind. and most
importantly, pay dues to karmic debt. i can't say the
same for you, but i'm ready to ascend. i'm ready to
be a hummingbird or a tree. i wanna be freer than
this lifetime's freedom. stuck no longer resonates. no
longer stuck in the matrix of distraction.

i wanna get out for good.

off course

you can never be who you're meant to be
if you're worried about how people
will view you every step of the way.

in tune

you ever look
inside yourself?

all bloody and blue
fluids done built up,
all the passion done grew.
you ever dig out the weeds,
dig out the bad things?
i think that's what we pose to do

gather the forest
the ever dying lull.

you ever have a green thumb?
know exactly what to work on?
you ever know the right ones to pick?

you ever rake out the leaves?
i think that's what we pose to do—

gather unconditional love for eve

for being curious enough.
for being honest enough.
for being such a woman.
such a passionate woman.
such a notorious woman

to be remembered, so harshly.
to be judged prematurely.

—you ever think that of you?
you ever wonder what they think?

me?   i wonder where this leads.
i wonder where this goes

i wonder do we find our power
after fully transitioning.
i wonder where eve goes.
i wonder if ever, she takes me.

i wonder if she takes me
—will i miss it here?

i bet, you'd miss the green
you miss the breeze
you miss the daze
you miss the ways of no worry
no responsibilities.

i bet you miss human things.

you ever protect yourself
from the outside world?
you ever sit alone
closed doors
in a zone?

you ever lock the war
outside?

_____

today, while i was writing
the war was outside.
the virus was spreading,
the love was gone.

i was looking for incense to burn.
i found one called "rain forest"
almost burnt it for you.
i thought—"but what if it manifests?"
        what if the rain
        spreads n spreads
        beyond the fire;
        beyond our being.

you ever concerned about the flood?
you ever find the flood arousing?
you ever look inside yourself?
all bloody and blue.

    you ever dig out
    the poison?

find the ruin,
find demons,
find fear?

new age

the matrix is draining
see-through, really
everyone wants to be
what the next person
wants to be
nobody likes the body
they were given
revisions unnatural
soul work on standby
the process stays
disrupted, mind
wandering.. spirit
wandering. no fulfillment
just satisfaction
temporarily. promise
land not always ripe
fruit and white roses.
sometimes you meet
heaven in the ugly things.
the matrix rejects
the ugly things so
i stand outside in
my truth undressed
        no mask on, no lies
this way
i learn, i see
who's dressed
the best

this is a sign to face
your addictions.
call them by their name.
take accountability
for the part you played,
and stay away for a while.

the sun

when people show you
themselves, believe 'em

blessings in disguise
god's favor on you

mirror staring back at you,
god's favorite tool

so now it's—
onto the next, shit,
before the demons
get too comfortable.

before the demons
multiply. one on top
of another, slow dancing
with yours. dirty dancing,
oh my.. eyes meeting eyes.
your eyes locked on mine.
what a blessing
to circle back
on a familiar love.
love this familiar
    keeps you
in the ring with god,
it keeps you resisting.
hesitant

look—reality is reality

the truth will never stop
showing its face

will never put a mask on.

do you care
about my well-being?
do you care
to ask me questions?
do you care
about my blessings

the way i
celebrate yours?

do you celebrate me?
do you celebrate me?

do you celebrate
me?

do you care
to ask me questions?
do you care
about my blessings
the way i
celebrate yours?
is your head high?

how high can
you take me?
can we fly?
can we float?

do you love me
enough to never
get too comfortable?

cause.. if not, it's
onto the next shit
'n onto the next

here's
to never settling.

here's
to confiding
within.

before it's too late

i forgive myself
for all the times
my intuition
tried to lead me
out of a toxic
situation and i
stayed thinking*
better would come.

new dawn

pray the bad blood
into blessings.
bless those
who got away.
water yourself
into a new day.
leave 'em
dying for thirst.

spirit message

the
bonds
you're
holding
onto have
expired.

what holds us?

it is your responsibility
to differentiate which
energies are for you
and which are working
against you. this doesn't
mean you have enemies
present, or on standby.
sometimes, these are
your loved ones. many
folk will deceive you.
will perceive themselves
to be a caregiver. will
give you poison in a
rose and not even
know the damage
from the thorns on
their own heart. the
truth evolves at last.
show them no mind.
show them love, still.

go blind

speak up
if you have to.
　　let it out
when you're ready.

only
if it makes you
　　feel—
only if you feel
called to share.

condolences
and check-ins
make me uneasy.

make
me
　　remember
too much
of what i want
to
forget.

let me
go blind

see through

self awareness is vital.
if you don't know yourself,
how can you recognize another?

my issue
is i'm always
missing
old versions
of people

the fool

don't ever let anyone
practice on you.
don't let them
prepare themselves
for the next thing.
don't be the demonstrator.
don't teach 'em about
the next life, if they're
halfway in this one.
don't ever be the fool

and if you do..
if you do,
don't hold yourself
from starting new.
there's larger mountains
there's fresher dew.
the skies clear as day
find a better view.
a greener green
a bluer blue.
something beautiful

start fresh.
start new
start new

and if you do..
if you do

won't you
be the fool
who—loves
harder

divine timing

watch what you say
when you speak to me

watch what you say
when you speak on me.

watch how you speak
when you speak about me
use your venom loosely.

obarra osa, what goes out
—will come back to you.

words won't prosper
the same
i promise
the downloads
go crazy

you are see-through.
i know you from before,
since before this life.

our bodies were one
our power—overkill.

we were cursed,
we were forced to separate.
our soul
split down the middle.
we were torn apart.

> *ever since,*
> *my soul has been*
> *searching for you.*

we came here
for each other
twin flame shit

it'd be a shame
it'd be a shame, truly,
to have to find out.

so, watch how you speak
when you speak about me

> use your venom loosely.

what goes out
will come back to you.
words won't prosper
the same

    i promise

i know you from before,
since before this life.

let the bells ring

when company
arrives i set
us both free.
take us on a ride
too intense
to sit quiet for.
our parents
didn't show us this.
didn't love like this.
i grant you
permission
to love on me
your hardest.
to touch on me
again. please do
that thing again
where you let
your guard down
and tell the truth.

please do
that thing
you do, where
you let me in
and you let me
love back on you.
our parents were
too afraid to love like this.

clarity

here's to manifesting
a new life. a clearer vision.
an abundant love.

here's to opening
our hearts to those
who need us, and
walking away from
places that serve us
no good.

here's to starting new,
without hesitation,
as often as change
requires us to.

beauty to me is faith.

some days, we can agree there is a god.
we've cried out for the same things.
in pain, in shame, in agony.
we've yelled out—in tears, with joy
with love, with grace.
we've made the same promise,
to be good.
so good, we repent.
we pray for both forgiveness
and freedom
from the mistakes we've made
we've lost our sense of conceit
we've lost our desire to be mortal
we wanna live with this moment forever.
things are good here.

—YOU—
where did you learn to be this good?

who did you speak to, to find me?
hide and seek,   it's possible
my demons sought out for you.

do you really believe you could love me?
do you really believe in a love
that could last forever?
do you—truly believe in
all ways?

you n me, we could pray on it.

we could talk to god together
ask 'em about the chances.
ask 'em to do us this solid,

say—just this once.
and believe it to be so.
and just believe
—we both believe in this
just as much, as one another.

beauty   to me,   is   faith.

at the end of the day,
i wanna say i do,
and believe you do, too.

bitter truth

if i believe you to be
the person, i know you can be
i will do my best to show
you yourself. i will hold you
up high, in the light of lights.

i will say i care,
in more ways than one.

if my words
are too bitter a medicine,
i will swallow them,
myself.

something tells me

sometimes you sit—
feel the sun on your lips, close your eyes,
feel the wind brush your nose and cheeks
feel your lashes sing.
you watch the clouds,
one by one. you say aloud,

"sit here."
"feel the moment."

you hum, out loud.
and you hum. and you hum.

sometimes—you
seek serenity.
sometimes you—
seek tranquility.

you think back to a happy place.
you sit in your memories.
you hug them with all you've got.
you say, "it's been a while."
you smile. you grasp the grass.
you breathe deeply.
you—snap back to reality.

something tells me you want to be loved—
you want to be touched intensely.
something tells me you hate it here
you hate waiting.
open to love // you wear your mask out of fear

you visit bars, visit parks
visit art walk shows.
nobody knows the real you
so you pretend.
god you pretend.

pretending to like the meals.
pretend to enjoy the night.
you say—tonight's the night i let loose.
you unwind
you *feel* yourself;
til you make it home alone.

something tells me
you're tired of making a home of your own
you wanna share space for once.

> well—i've been holding space for you
> i wanna love you.

sometimes i wanna sit.
i wanna nitpick your attributes..
i wanna love you in your language.
i'll say, "let's look up at the sky . . .
i want us to look in each other's eyes
while the moon is lit."
i'll say, "let's count our blessings,
i'll go first.

    god,
    help me protect this man.
    help me keep him near.
    our souls at unity
    at one with each other.
    our bond is rare,
    i'm blessed—
    i don't sleep on that"

then i'll ask you, "where do you go?"
"when you're inside your head."
"are you away from me there?"
"are you still playing pretend?"
"do you wait for me there?"
"do you wonder where i go
when i'm nowhere near?"

sometimes i seek serenity
sometimes i seek tranquility
i think back to a happy place.
i sit in my memories
i hug them with all i've got.
i say.. it's been a while
i smile. i grasp the grass;
i breathe deeply.

my dreams are my reality.

and beyond

i'm not ashamed
to grow old
to pile dust
throughout my wings
to fall short
once i get up to fly

i'm not afraid to fall ill
to ache all over
if it's true
i've lived a life
full of laughter

i'm not swayed
by the common things
i desire a love that dips
seven feet deep; feelings
too obscure to make out

i'm not saying
i'm not apprehensive
about what's on the other side;
i'm saying, you give me
the courage to commit

and, when you're ready to go
somewhere beyond here, and this,
i'd love to come with.

nectar of life

i have no desire
to journey
in a rush.

all the sweet
things in life
come
when you're
sitting still

funny like that

last summer, i spent my days at home.
stuck inside, stuck in the middle of wifey
and mom life things.   stuck in love
with the way things were moving.
i was truly okay with the calm.   i was okay
with birthing new things, i was learning
how to give my all—to a new life,
this was a new thing. i—spent my time
swinging in my backyard,
overlooking the valley view.

overthinking, about whether
i was doing a good job or failing.

i cried at the thought of miscarrying you.
misleading you like they did me.

they left me to fend for my own,
teaching me love isn't a victory.
teaching me that family is a
made up thing, you've only
got your impulse. you can
only trust the moment. there
isn't much to look forward to.
so i've never looked forward.

i just wanna do the right thing.

i wanna expose you to an
honest, healthy life—i wanna
love you in a new way. i
wanna show you how to hold
someone. i wanna show you
how it feels to be held. i wanna
show you how it feels to be
welcomed—flaws and all.

so i sat with you. i learned
your language. *i learned patience.*
i learned how to sit silent.
i learned—nothing was ever
fully about me. i'm only the vessel.

last summer i learned to love.

despite my feelings, despite myself..
i woke up every hour
to make sure you were
breathing correctly.
i came near, just
to hug you tighter.
just to let you know
i was there. i waited
for you to wake up
i put you first.
naturally, i put me
second. i don't regret it.

but so
last summer, i lost ahold of myself.
self care slipped right out from underneath
my fingertips. i forgot the meaning
of downtime. i forgot how to laugh.
how to say i need help, without guilt.

so i sat with you
i spoke your language
i heard your voice for the first time.
i sat with patience.
i listened.

i listened when you told me,
"i am not trying to be a burden."

i listened when you said
you are here to make me happy.

i heard you make it clear,
you said "hi,   my name is umi."
you mentioned us being soulmates.
you said, "nice to meet you."
you said, "take your time.
i will love you—regardless."

"take your time
i will love you.
regardless."

do you promise?

often we speak
about holding
ourselves
accountable
when we are wrong
—but how?

do you show up?
do you reach out?
do you apologize?

do you swallow your pride
and set your ego to the side?

do you own up
to how you were wrong?
in every which way?
do you promise
not to do the same,
again?

you stunt your growth
when spirit calls you
to do a different kind
of work than you're used to
—and you decide not to,
out of fear.

light work

you have to remind yourself
to take a break from doing
"the work" sometimes.
remind yourself that it'll be
there when you get back.
remind yourself that
you are human, you are fragile,
you are tired—sometimes
you need a moment alone,
to love on yourself.

miscarriage

yesterday
i could see
your heartbeat.

thump
after thump.

today
i am bleeding.
wasting away.

shaming
this flesh.

beating
my heart.

questioning
my soul.

have i ever
been good
enough?

have i ever
been worthy?

spirit says

cry today.
there's a load
in your back.
there's a brick
on your chest.
there's heavy weight,
everywhere.
from point,
to point, to point—
healing hands are needed.
rough hands are needed.

you weren't built
to house this damage.

each corner
full of clutter,
each wall
painted with filth,
the unspoken kind.

spirit says,
you've done a swell job,
getting this far along.
finding doors
with no mess behind them.
creeping through doors
not meant for you.

spirit says,
you're encouraged
to cry today.

my old lady

i have regret
here with me,
chilling right
beside me.
resting at the
end of my bed.

we don't talk
much, we just
sit together. we
run our errands,
we take our bath.
we hold hands
as we climb up
in love, or in lust
—it's the ladder
that saves us.

the higher
the better.
the grey in the
sky resembles
true fate.
i have regret
here with me.
—i guess you
could say
we go together.

good woman

today i'm taking
a moment for myself.
sharing testimony,
or a testament.

here, things are lonely.
let me be the precedent
things.. are not good here.
i say this while suffering,
fighting, denying,
expiring; hoarding apologies
to myself from others.

protecting my truth
from falling on deaf ears
protecting what's true
from falling short.
nursing distress.
feeding fears to the soul.
i resent me for it.

i'm protecting these blues
like they've been miscarried
like—i carry 'em best.
like—i held 'em
healthy this time

i think they're fine here.

i save angst in my chest,
in my lungs, in my gut
i save it just in case—
i force it in a fragile place.

who better to keep it safe?

i can keep the guilt away
tucked, hidden
behind dirty habits
and foggy glasses
and tears on tears
on journeys that never
let you forgive yourself
only distract you
for the moment.
sunsets, that remind you:
i forgot to smoke.
here, *hit that shit*
write another.
inhale, then
let it out this time.

i wrote this letter.
in the evening.
i stood up til midnight,
during a busy time
to say "you matter."
no matter how empty.
no matter how grim.

i felt i owed myself notice
for forgetting—me.
i casually
put everyone first
    even when it hurt
     i bit the bullet.
talked my way out of
speaking up. speaking out
talked my way out of saying,
  "it's been difficult to breathe easy."

on the road toward mercy—
i cried. i yelled. i wept.
i held myself in private.
during car rides, showers,
singing, cleaning, and cooking;
i forced myself to feel.
i unpacked my pride
hoping no one could see me
i felt ashamed
i felt my angels talking
saying, "speak up."
saying, "speak up."
saying, "you have to figure out
how to keep up with this life!"
"you have to get it together."
so i tried to get right.
tried to go out.
tried to have fun.
i didn't know how to.

i was too tired. i was too worried.
i was too insecure. i didn't know my body,
i didn't like her. told her she's no good.
told her she let me down.
'n i just kept on
and i kept on
and i kept on feeling terrible
i kept feeling exhausted
so

// i wrote myself
this letter to say:

    step back.

i wrote myself this letter
to say step back.
everything will turn out okay
you don't always
have to be in control.

trust the people
around you,
they got this.
they got you.

truly,
you need a break
cause you're breaking here.

i receive it

deep breaths
back to little ones
i watch the time go by.

i can't hold on to yesterday
i can't bring it with me,
i can only learn from it.

"how to be more happy?"
        // to be less worried.
        i ask, and i receive.

deep breaths,
back to little ones
i meditate on it.

i can't hold on to yesterday
i can't bring it with me,
i can only learn from it.

"how to be less worried?"
        // to be more accepting.
        i ask, and i receive.

i trust the message for what it is.
 i trust in all i receive.
i can't hold on to yesterday.
i can only learn from it.

someone else

"i am not like her
enough.
i am not as pretty
i am not as petite
i am not as special
i am not as holy."

we tell ourselves
these things.

we believe
these things
to be true

we believe we aren't
deserving of the same.

we beat
ourselves
down,
we wear
ourselves out

——we create a monster.

scorpio moon

this is the one
where i let
my guards down.

i say the things
most people
don't know about.

cancer mercury—
i tell a feeling,
not a story.

i talk my shit
i let it loose
i let yaw know
i see it so vividly.

the real shit
that matters.

disloyalty
is a quality
i don't relate to.

all the funny activity,
all the weirdos.
all the, "whenever you need me,
i'm here for yous"
i really don't trust
a living soul.

maybe my
scorpio moon's
to blame.

i connect
with
transitioned
people.

i ask them,
"am i insane?"

i do what they
ask because i
appreciate the
open
communication.

    they bless me more.

i really don't trust
a living soul.

i woke up
too many days
having to fight
the cold on my own.

i woke up
too many nights
having to fight
bad thoughts,
having to persuade
myself i'm not
out here on my own.

blessedness

what do you
feed your insides?
what kinda food?

karma recreates itself

make sure
it's the truth.

speak with intention.
speak from a place
of tribute.

ground your feet
into the world
they gave us.

find your place, 'n
grow roots there.

watch your moods!
watch your moods!
watch
your moods!

these are
the tools to
wellness.

forgive me

right now i'm sitting here,
thinking to myself,
"which level are you on?"

might be too high.
might be too vulnerable.
i think, "are you vulnerable
enough to tell the truth?"

it's true, the truth hurts.

the truth leaves you
scarred sometimes.

makes you it's bitch.

keeps you scared
of sharing,   so i'll start here

for the person
i've been dreaming
of all my life:
i've been a bitch lately,
ain't been true to you.
ain't been fair to you.

haven't been the one
that you chose.
—i've been through the mud,
'n i've been blaming you.

don't share the pain
with no one else
　　keep you out the loop.

say i—got no real love.
say i got nothing good.
even when,
you've only ever been
good to me.

　　our calamity
　　is my fault.

i hold on to the very most.
i do the most, and for what?
nothing will ever　be that serious.

i'm just
fighting demons who're
fighting the healing.

too many demons
trying to heal around me.
　　too many evil eyes,
　　disguised
　　as love.

i'm ashamed—i ever put you second.

lotus

love is love is love is love
one day i'll talk about
how you grew me up.
pulled me up.
showed me how
when the sun is up
we put prayers up.

we keep our spirits lifted
even when
the light starts shifting.
we praise the rain
just as often as the sunshine.

we hold each other—
we show spirit
we know love.

we show spirit
that all the hate formed
against our love
would never
and could never prosper.

we praise the most high
for a love like this.
we praise the most high
for every deep experience.

it takes a different kind of
strength to know the value over
your life. to never settle for less.
to trust that god will place you
in all the appropriate places,
when the timing is right.

wheel of fortune

my cup runs over
and over,
and over again.

you will not find me
half empty,
or half full.

my hard work
pays off

my mouth
never stays
parched for long.

i never ask for a thing,
i sit patient.

don't do
the hard work
for a pay out

i just stay
out the way
and trust mine.

Grandma Theresa

my abuelita said "como estas?"
she said, how
come i never
hear from you
anymore?
she goes, tell
everyone don't
cry for me
when i'm gone,
because no one
came to visit
while i was
still here. she
said, and how's
life? i bet good,
since you don't
worry about
anyone but
yourself. she said,
and how's sleep?
i bet well, since you
don't seem to miss any.
   she goes—don't
forget how much
i took care of you.
remember when
your mom used
to work all those
jobs and i'd watch
you for hours.

don't forget i
was there for you.
you remind me of
her so much. you
just go off and
do your own thing.

y tu? you forget
about me. you
don't worry if
i'm lonely. you
don't worry if
i'm healthy. entonces,
86 and i still send
a prayer up. i still
pay my dues. i
know you're of
blood—so i know
my responsibility.
still, i think of you.
i hold you in my
heart so you're always
near.   and your
mother, we used to
be connected by the
hip. but you know
how she can be.
tell her to call me please.
la extraño mucho.
i shouldn't have

to go chasing.
i've become tired.

so.. le digo a mi mamá. and she
say nothing.. of course
but i wonder, was i
programmed this
way? was i trained
to look out for
myself and no one
else? was i meant to
be alone? did i make
any mistakes thinking
i could live a life of
my own. you know,
creating a family of
my own. having a
son to look after. to
love after. sharing
love with a person
who doesn't fully
get me. knowing
parts of me, he'll
never fully know.
having someone
always wonder the
thoughts in my
head—whenever
i sit silent. did i
think this through?

i look at my mom.
i wonder the
thoughts in her
head. i wonder if
i was a mistake. i
wonder if she knew
she wasn't capable.
i wonder if my
father was her capacity.

i tell her,
"abuela dice que te extraña."

"she says if you
can call her."

my mom says nothing.
i say   nothing back.

i think . . .   "maybe next time."

tourism

my daddy did
a number on me
shit, my mama, too

"thorough"
ain't the word
it's through
and through

through the battles
through warfare
through whatever
it takes to evolve.
it's forever. until
then, and even after.

it's we get each other
it's we got each other

it's a reason we
keep coming back.
it's a reason we
keep showing up.
coincidence can't
be the foundation
i believe in.
there must be an
agreement somewhere.

a contract so
rich, we pull up
every time.

one day i'll
meet the real.
i'm tryna discern
who chose who?
did you need me
or did i need you?

i'm roaming through
the portals wondering.
my travels are
getting hella deep.

i remember too much.
i remember too much.
i remember too much
bad shit that had to do
with you. my mentor
Ciaryn told me—we
were rivals repeatedly.
one life after another.

she said we still
got a few more
to go til we reach
true harmony
—see you then

and so

at times i hide myself
until i'm forced to release
old versions grow old,
no good—too soon
sooner than
i prepare to leave.

be patient with your journey.

tears will come, let them.
friends will go, let them.
love will bloom..
or fade,   let it.

the more you clean house
the more you open space
for new life and new blessings
to settle in.
take each day—one by one.

antibodies

this is an interlude
this is progression
this is where the
rapture meets us
unpretty, iffy, empty,
as honest as can be
fear lives down the
street from you and me
in the home with the
most traction. see the
action lives for free.
right there at the
corner where deception
smiles back. the joint
where dark clouds
recruit. and the breeze—
oh the breeze says hello.
has a spell brewing
asks all the right
things to seem a way.
i avoid these places.
the faces wear scary
eyes. don't greet
sound people with
love and life.
judas stays dressed
up in his finest.
speaks the same
language, but
don't take pride

in it. must not
hear it the same.
words flowing tho
jive sings in tunes
dreadful rendezvous.
the ones who attach
themselves to the
memory of discomfort
cripple themselves.
if the end is near
they won't make
it there. and damn
right you will
cross paths as
you wait in line
for your turn. they
will distract you
right where you are,
they will promise you
things you cannot
resist, they will give
you an illusion
in return for your
spirit. your sweet
sweet spirit. your
innocent self. they
will trap you
in the moment.

May 27th 2020

today feels heavy as fuck!

you ever seen a nigga get kilt?
you ever been the killer?
you ever point fingers
instead of surrender?

you ever resist?
you know what resisting feels like for us?
        giving up.

you know what giving up feels like for us?
           murder.

feels like—it's been forever since
we let too much slide.
been ill-fated ever since.
been on the wrong side of luck,
on the wrong side of saved.

guess we should've prayed more
guess we should pay our dues   more
shoulda gave thanks more
should've said a word—

you ever seen a nigga shout?
seen a nigga get dealt the cards
he was given?

still walk around—
mind on earth
body in prison.

[here i'm inserting the filtered version]
don't wanna scare the folk
who pretend to love me.

[here i'm inserting the truth.]
i'm elevating my grandfather right now.
lighting a candle for 9 days straight.
he served in the US MILITARY
for 9 whole years
i can't even find him on google.

i'm tired of watching my own
fade away. we are disposable to them.
they don't care about our bodies
once our magic is forgotten.

today feels heavy as fuck.

today feels like i been here before.
today feels like routine.
today feels like death.
today feels   like death.

today feels like death
tonight   feels like war   is coming.

circle back

heartbreak
after heartbreak,
heart never
finding its way
back to full.

void of course

i am a woman
whose father is a black man.

i am a woman
raising a black man.

i am a woman
who is in love with a black man.

i am a woman
who loves on black men.

i am a black woman
who bears the weight
of us both.

who is harder to love.

my complexion
thrown back at me.
the skin on my body.
the melanin on my face.
it's color. it's shade.

so for now i mark "other."
you see, the world
advocates for womxn.
loves to go on and spew
about our strength.

black men in power
—feminists, they say.
we should all
be feminists, they say.
we should ride
'til the wheels fall off.

the black men
in our lives,
they love them
some black women.

doesn't stop them
from cheating.
doesn't stop them
from leaving
when the war begins.

the black men
in our lives,
they love them
some black women.

doesn't stop them from
raising their voice.
doesn't stop them
from reminding us
our grace stems from silence.
our voice runs void,
our feelings senseless
or out of place.

the black men
in our lives, sure..
they LOVE women.

but won't support
our kind the same way.
won't respect us the same.

      they won't deal
      with too much.

i seen it up-close
when my daddy said
—don't follow them.
don't learn from them.
don't copy their habits,
you're different.

almost as if he were
giving me permission
to judge the women
who looked like me.
almost as if he were
judging me.. almost,
as if he were saying
neglect this side.
almost as if he were
saying don't look like them.
don't look toward them.
don't let them be the influence.

i seen it up-close
when my daddy said
don't be like them,
you're different.

i seen the trauma pour out.

the black women
in his life,
always let him down.
so he put a face
on disappointment
and labeled it a black woman.

he chose to suffer
somewhere else.
somewhere nude toned.
somewhere unfamiliar.

i seen it up close
when my daddy
chose to suffer
in the arms of a
woman WE tried
to save him from.

**if my concern is offensive
we are better off at a distance.
i cannot love in any other way.**

in general

toxicity has no face.
abuse has no face.
trauma has no face.
manipulation
can breed in anyone.
manipulation
can damage anyone.

tables turn

it's hard to keep your silence
when you're tempted not to.
never was the type to share
my feelings off rip. a lot of
heartbreak in this world.
a lot of heartbreak around the
world. a lot of losing our heroes.

black women
make the world go round
—can make shit stop, too.

what power

what power
do the men hold
if they cannot convert our
beliefs without force?

what power
do the men hold
if they cannot
birth a single thing?

butterflies

it takes a million deaths
to reach your full potential.
it takes a million lives
to get it right.

good thing

the good thing is—
you still give me that feeling.

you still make me long.
i think, how could he be content
without me? for this long?

i check your page.
is he safe? is he incomplete?
do his new "thing" value him
the way he's supposed to be.
you know.. the way one's
supposed to value the person
they've been dreaming of all
their life. i mean one can dream
right?   hope shit cool.
all the lights out,
all the music gone—
i wander. i wonder
how you dance to our song;
does it have the same meaning?
i ponder—if you're being seen
the way you're supposed to.
is the story of love being shared
the way i do. i can admit,
it's been too many times
where i do too much.
i'm about tired of
sharing about what
this was you think

i'm still bragging
about us. i see you
peep it every time,
i see you peep me
every time. i know you
love the attention
you know i was never
sure about you tho.
never tapped in
the way we thought
we would. we never really
grew to know each other.
never really grew together.
chemistry so fire——we just
understood. it's no deep
conversation about
what
is love

or what love is

we..   we just do what feels nice
what you think feel right?

never mind the labels,
the drama, the expectations
never mind the rules
we do the things we like
never mind,
i always get too caught up.

// i see you
still write for me.
still seeking attention
in dramatic ways. you never
shared your heart in emphatic
ways.
always takes the static
for you to cave in.
every few months
we touch base, you
give me time to grow
into a newer me.
you write for the newer
me to respond to.
you test the climate.
    is it hot or cold?
have my ways grown
sad and old? are the games
still exciting?
back when i first
pulled up on you
—you were waiting
arms intertwined.
crossed tight, "let's chill"
playing lightly in the background.
i looked up, seen you smiling.
seen you hiding it.
red wine set the vibe,
read the vibe so clearly.
you were mine, then.

did you know
you were mine then?

let 'em know
you were mine then.

i wore all black this night
the white lights
too blinding.
the red light hides you,
guides conversation
i see you wanna
know too much,
you wanna hold
and touch the sun
just for fun, yet..
you know better.

the good thing is
i never took you
too serious. knew
you were just as
lost as i was. just
as curious. curious if
i had that thing,
that drug, that feeling.
i'm curious..
do i still give you that feeling?
when i cross your mind,
when you find your way to mine,

when you realize you could never
leave me lone.   is it for the good things?
is it cause you remember how good
it felt when we were laughing, when
we were dancing, when we were
searching deeper than deep. you know,
you know what's up. don't play.
you knew eye was too radical for you.
too raw for you.   too celestial.

it's a good thing you kept your distance.
it's a good thing i kept mine. knew
the right time would never come.
would never find its way.   it's too bad

the good thing is we
had a good thing going.
kept good shit flowing
'til the very end. til
shit started to get too real.

you know it's too bad
you say you've moved on
but you're still writing about me.

still waiting for the right time.

you know shit real.

you know shit real

when you ask the sun
when you ask the moon
when you pray to the stars
about me..
lemme ask you—

what is it about me?

when's the last time
you gave yourself
the flowers you deserve?

get lucky

you will never find
another like me.
not another day
not another year
not another time.
not any life but this one.

let's talk about
limitless and infinite
let's talk about
trauma bonds
let's talk about
bonding over
pain or all the work
it took to get here.
you still let me
down in the process.

you still overlooked me.

lied to my face
about other bitches
and what y'all said
between each other.
about how long
you've known each other.
lied to my face
about your feelings.
i guess that's the
real kind of love

what that is they say?
        you not in real love
if you don't lie to protect
your loved ones' feelings?

i never understood 'til now.

but i could still
never trust you for it.

and i still could
never leave you
for it neither.

this here is a different
story of love to tell.

i love you in places
i've never loved myself.
i love you in places
i could never love myself.

you will never find
another like me.
not another day
not another year
not another time.
not any life   but this one.

envy

watch how quick
people switch on you
when they start
to feel threatened.

saying grace

it's a good day
to move on
good luck
and good
riddance.

sunday blues

it's been a month
since i've written.
i've been hitting
blank after blanks.
it's 9 in the morning,
i decide i'll take
a shower now.
i'll cleanse this
feeling away. that's
what you'd want.

i can hear your voice,
louder now—than ever.
i can hear you say,
"little girl.   don't play with me."

you knew
my power
before i did.

you loved me deep
you made me
feel everything.

sometimes rage,
sometimes pain
sometimes mighty
sometimes like treasure.
nothing less
than gold.

you built
my bones.
held me
up high.
all that strength,
all that fight.

gave me
a hard head.
gave me
a loud mouth.
gave me spirit.

i told spirit,
send me love.
send me love.
send me love.

let me know..
i need an ETA.
i need
to breathe again.
i need; i need to see her.

i need to know
she's okay.

did she make it safe?
can she
see me still?
can she
hold me still?
slow me down?
sit me down?
give me a hug?

can she
call me
again?

sunday.
i love you fool.
i miss you fool.

you said..
you were
staying..

you promised.
you promised.
you promised.
you promised.

you promised.
you promised.
you promised.
you promised.

you promised.
you promised.
you promised.
you promised.

you promised.
you promised.
you promised.
you promised.

you promised.
you promised.
you promised.
you promised.

you promised.
you promised.
you promised.
you promised.

my fault

your last words
to me were
"fine, i'll go."

your hair a mess,
two days prior,
your legs had given out.

your poor
foggy memory.
skimming generations,
new and old.

you were too tired
to fight. you saw
things we couldn't.

a beautiful life, beyond this one.

a bright luminescent light,
a welcome home party.
you saw your nana's
big smile. you heard
your daddy say
he's on his way.
you couldn't wait
to meet them.

your last words
to me were
"you look so pretty!
where you going?"

maybe if i would
have asked the same,
i would've asked you
to stay home,
with me instead.

summer time

summer time ain't nothing special without sunday,
praise and worship, hopping on neighborhood
buses—shouting "what's poppin?!" out the window.
soul food and jesus come to save the day. pot of
gumbo stacked out the rim, crab legs as long as our
blessings. we count 'em over. we say thank you for
the day the lord has made. a choir singing the same
song. waiting for our chance to be chosen. who will
tell the first story? who will make 'em laugh the
most?   the women in our family ain't that easy to
impress. broken hearts put up around the house, gold
medallions. i wonder how talented you have to be to
forget loss after loss? i wonder how strong—do you
have to be to carry the burden on each shoulder. you
apologize for having weak shoulders, you apologize
for accepting the exhaustion.. when they are already
amazed of your skills to keep going. already plotting
on your downfall. already setting up shop. still, you
apologize for having empathy. you apologize for
forgiving and forgiving. having no cold bone in your
body.   you apologize
for having so much fire.

summer time ain't nothing without laughter. them
long random calls be the best ones. be busy as shit
but still know your obligation. when love comes
calling, you answer back. when loyalty falls in your
lap, you say thank you. you let god see your colors.
you show the women back home you appreciate
the guides you've got for now. they speak at you,

wondering what the hold up is—wondering when
you'll come visit. you say a joke or two to shift the
light of focus, because you don't recognize the
abundance. and they laugh. and they applaud. they
understand your position. so they loosen their grip
because it's too tight. and it's too soon to wake you
up. to summon you back. the women back home just
want to laugh too.
wanna play with you sometimes. wanna say hello.

   hummingbirds come to visit

one with a sea-foam tail, sucking the sweet
nectarine out a firebush tree with coral tips,
singing toward the sunshine.

feel the sun

one ten around midday,
i see you in all your sadness,
i open my arms,
i wave,   "over here!"

summer time is when we get the chance
to say "hello" back. sunday reminds us
to say "hello" back. we don't miss our call.
we wake up early, just in case.
we wake up early just to say thank you to the sun.
we wake up early to say thank you to god
for every giving sunday, in the summer time.

spirit guide

sitting in a cool room,
on a hot day in october.
eyes as pink as sunsets
on a warm night in july.
eyes watering all the plants
i retain. memory bringing
what's dead—back alive.

i wish it was
a physical metaphor.
the kind of manifestation
all the cards predict
i am to have. i manifest
your being here. i feel you
in the corner. i feel you
in my sleep. i feel you
by the hour, by the minute.

four by four by four.

thank you
for your blessing
i receive it.

six by one by eight,
i know   you're demanding
to get through.
i'm trying to listen.
our angels gather around,
put their force together

spark up light
pull from source
connect us
to raise my awareness.

they do the most
they show out

they go the extra mile—
they'd do that for you.

—

and (you) go
the extra mile
to let me know, once again

how loved   i am,   still.

you'd do that for me.

i know it.

be kind to your elders

a lot of our grandmothers
were witches, and theirs, and theirs.
they must have been ambushed
or bullied, they were too scared
to claim medicine as their own.
too traumatized to even think
about it.

do you know their ghosts
have hunted after us for
many many years? wasn't til
now they found a way through.
        wasn't til—me and you.

be kind to your elders
they will come looking

yes they will come looking,
for you.

greed is an ugly seed
to plant.

fate calls on us

there's a thing
time won't fix
a black hole
too deep

an ache that sits
and sits and sits

stings a bit.

can't make no
wrong moves

no wrong turns

every flaw disrupts
the system. it takes
a village to lift us
swing us into rhythm
our ancestors'
tunes come on

turn it up.
turn it up.

loud enough
to hear the
lowest of notes
to feel the deepest
of feels.
even if, you feel sick
to your stomach
we dance and
we surrender.

fate calls on us.

we can survive
the soreness
we can do this
like the women before.

i will hold your weight
if you will support mine.

we can cry together
we can laugh after

in this moment we learn
healing looks a lot messier
than they will tell you.

what makes you happy?

the same things that make me sad.

universe

i built an altar
on the shelf right
at the side of my bed.
i long for; i thirst for
commitment and
communication.
i rub my hands
together to create
warmth. the fire
dances as i approach
it. my ears ring
through the cosmos.
strikes a nerve
throughout; my
muscles sore. this is
a different weight
lifting. i learn to
exchange dreams.
i learn to exchange
stillness. i notice
angels running
in the dark. to
give me a signal
or symptoms
or spasms. to learn
me an ascension.
ghosts in gurus.
or vice versa—   i learn a new thing.

to be continued

i give in order
to get back. i give
praise before i
inquire about the
stuff that requires
plenty of energy.
i ask

am i in
the right place?
is this the right
place for me?

should i be
moving on,
doing greater
things?

is there someone
out there who
might give me
safer feelings
than you do?

like voodoo.
i'm too spent
on the high of life.
need a drug to bring me down.
bring me to
my senses,

it's true..
i expect too much.
i need
the highest form.
i need the highest form.
i need the highest
form of love.

i need euphoria.

i think of
the strangest things,
maybe i'm here to love
love, don't mean
we got it tho.
could i be missing
my blessing? or
dodging a bullet? idk.

the other day
i said goodbye
for the last time.
your demons
brang out the evil eye.
showed me a thing or two.
showed me what i knew
already.

silly me

i forgive myself
for all the times
i fell in love
with a person
who was
emotionally
unavailable
to begin with.

not today,
not tomorrow

"i love you"
means nothing to me.

not the same thing
as proof

pour out

grief is an upside down,
all around kind of thing.
you never know when it's gone.
you don't even know where it began.
you just keep collecting.
hoarding ache on top of ache.
saving cry on top of cry.
you tell yourself, "when i'm alone."
you tell yourself, "later on."
you say, "soon. i'll release it."
yeah.. soon—i'll release it.
 still, you crave silence and the dark.
you hold sadness close by,
don't even realize its hold on you.
you wake up feeling heavy
everyday, can't figure out
where all the extra weight
came from. but shit, you stay high.
you tighten up. wear a smile if you must.
force yourself out of bed—
face yourself outta bed.
the last standing hope.
ready to make a move.
you swear you're on a journey toward
freedom. swear you're on the right path.
somehow, you swear
you gon' find joy without dealing
with the healing shit.
 see, grief is an upside down
—all around kind of thing.

nothing pretty.
you learn the hard way.
you learn suffering.
you learn you can't move on
and you can't move forward
until you let the pain move around
your space for a while.
give your thoughts room.
invite her energy. ask the blue
to make herself at home.   watch..
watch how she open up the blinds one day.
let the sun see your tears for once.
let the moon see your tears.
say your prayer toward the light.
let spirit hear what your heart says.
let the light fill you.

you hold onto it long enough,
it starts to pour out.

you hold onto it long enough,
it starts to pour out.

you hold onto it long enough,
        it'll pour out.

let it live in you,
then let it go without you.

when you purge

you lose weight,
you lose ego,
you lose friends,
you lose concentration
on what's unfulfilling.

you cry
til you can't anymore.

spirit washes
all the unnecessary out,

whether you signed up
for the cleanse, or not.

florida waters

i done aged like
triple times over
since the world
shut down. gifts
offering relief
and stress at once.
i get us all free.
bones ache
throughout
my body. red rum
medley. i see red
runs in the family.
the problem is
our ways of life.
demon shit.
the fire will keep us
busy or wipe us out.
this is a blessing
depending on who
you spread it to.
murder she sowed.
murder, she worried,
would not be an escape.
the life after this
one, there's no
guarantee. roots go
deep. grandma
planted them
heartbreaks
in the grounds

that're blessed or
hexed by murky
bodies of water.
florida sweet,
the humidity
reminds me of
a life i used to live.
comfortably
uncomfortable.

some nights are
heavy on me. drifting
between one realm
and another for
the remedies
to almost anything.
my shoulder pays
the price. eyes lower
by the second.   sunday
reminds me not
to forget her water.
i place sweet potatoes 'n
greens in her special bowl.
protection candles
burn a new flame.

i say grace
a triple times over

meeting joy

transitioning
from grief
to grateful.

tribe

in all ways
i am the
women who
came before.
i am the
children who
grow after.
many of
journeys
marrying,
both, play
and wisdom.

new visitors

my people
don't die
real deaths.

they come
in different
forms—again
and again.

make peace

no one is 'yours'
no one is 'yours'
no one is 'yours'
no one is 'yours'
no one is 'yours'
no one is 'yours'
no one is 'yours'
no one is 'yours'
no one is 'yours'
no one is 'yours'
no one is 'yours'
no one is 'yours'
no one is 'yours'
no one is 'yours'
no one is 'yours'
no one is 'yours'
no one is 'yours'
no one is 'yours'
no one is 'yours'
no one is 'yours'
no one is 'yours'
no one is 'yours'
no one is 'yours'
no one is 'yours'
no one is 'yours'
no one is 'yours'
no one is 'yours'
    to be held onto
    forever.

in waves

do you know
how beautiful
it is to be aware?
to be thankful
for your life?
to understand
the privilege
to be free, both
mentally and
physically?
do you know
how beautiful
it is to walk
with intention?
to move with
pure intentions?

do you know
how beautiful
the karma
could be if you
kept your thoughts
to yourself?

do you know
how beautiful
it is to not
overshare?
to not care
too much

about people
who don't give
a fuck.   now—
i don't give
a fuck neither.

do you know
how beautiful
it is to pay the
bills off happiness?
to never have
to work hard
for people who're
undeserving?
whose spirits
don't mesh well
with mine?

do you know
how lucky you
are, how blessed
you are, how
chosen you are
to be living your
truth? how's your truth
looking? don't like
the outcome?

destiny manifests
energy multiplies

sometimes too fast
for our liking
sometimes
too slow. you can't
rely on time
to mend blatant
wounds. what you
push toward
the dark
will ruin you.

karma don't
miss nobody

karma don't
miss no body.

do you know
what it means
to be happy?
do you know
what happiness
looks like for you?
do you pay
attention to
the details?
do you recollect?

do you retrace
your steps
when you
feel alone?

do you ever
wonder
what's missing
when you
feel alone?
   is it someone?
   is it something?

are you missing
someone?
or are you missing
      something?

these are questions
you ask when
you're mindful of
your existence.

do you know
how beautiful it is,
to stay accountable?

'n do you know
how beautiful it is,
to be aware?

spring cleaning

give what you can
afford to. give
what you won't
miss. give until
you can't no more.

honey child

i drizzle honey
on pineapples
i offer my folk
the sweetest
of sweet.

good grief

sometimes you miss a feeling
you'll never meet again; a bond
that could never be recreated.
hits twice as deep when they loved
you more. when unconditional
is the only name to give them.

clockwork

God says,
>   "i love you back"

spirit says,
>   "i love you back"

our ancestors say,
>   "i love you back"

the angels say,
>   "i love you back"

our guides say,
>   "i love you back"

the birds say,
>   "i love you back"

our parents say,
>   "i love you back"

the trees say,
>   "i love you back"

they could never
unlearn you. they
could never know
love, without you.

join me

i connect with honesty

i connect with pain
i connect with addiction

i connect with gratitude

i connect with fear

i connect with heartbreak

i connect with HUNGER
i connect with frugality

i connect with mental dis—ease

i connect with humanity
i connect with hope

i connect with love.

i do not condemn nor judge
the next man for his experience.
it is not my place—i am no better.

i empathize and celebrate,
WHOEVER, through whatever.

forever more

it's some deaths you grieve forever.
a couple lost ones you miss everyday.

my issue
is i'm always
missing
old versions
of myself

dead weight

a lot of our suffering
comes from our attachment
to what is no longer.
when you find pleasure
in the moment,
when you say
"okay. this is my life now
and i accept it."
it isn't until then
that you find peace
it isn't until then
that you're truly able to breathe
and let go

see you

it takes a certain kind of wisdom to understand your
responsibilities—here on earth. it takes a certain
kind of awareness to guide yourself away from
repeating cycles. a certain kind of power to cut
the cords attached to you. but really, the most
important thing is to mind your business. keep
from judging others.
it harms you; it troubles you. ask your guides to limit
your troubles. it is okay to grieve our lost ones, it is
okay to be brokenhearted.. but in order to fulfill the
souls of our ancestors, we MUST live FULLY.
we must take risks. we must love HARD! share
your heart. pour your love in everything. we must
forgive and move on. no grudges held.
this is how our ancestors rest easy.

live your life to its fullest.
honor those who honor you.

i'm not self righteous, i'm self aware.
i've been the fool, plenty
—but you learn from that.
i've been angry many of days
—but you learn from that.

you make it out.

here's to progress:
we still have a lot to learn.

"human being > human doing"

"the North Node occurs in our birth chart directly
opposite of our South Node. it is determined at
the time of birth by the exact position of the sun,
moon, and earth. it represents what someone's soul
came to learn in a lifetime that will bring them out
of their comfort zone. this astrological placement is
a secret to living your best most meaningful life. the
North Node is meant to be your path in 'this life'
and the South Node is the door that you
came through."

find yours.
learn yours.
live yours through.